Introduction

GW00891704

The concept of cyberspace is difficult to grasp and yet, paradoxically, the internet is rapidly becoming a large part of our everyday existence. Website addresses adorn all manner of advertisements, magazines and television shows have on-line entities to complement their print and broadcast offerings. Services and utilities exhort us to pay their bills by BPay over the phone or over the internet. The banks, and even the phone companies, are promising us discounts if we opt to visit them on line, rather than in person. And it seems to be all our kids and newsreaders talk about.

So why, you're asking yourself, is the internet any good to me? Isn't it all just more trouble than it's worth? Another reason to stay trapped in front of my computer instead of getting out into the fresh air?

Absolutely not. The internet, despite its bad press and apparent complexity, can be fun, challenging and, above all, extremely useful. This book serves as an introduction to something more amazing and far-reaching than you could ever have imagined. Welcome to the web.

WE'VE COME A LONG WAY...

Strange but true. Back in 1993, when the internet was still gaining currency and access was restricted to universities and people "in the know", a popular place to visit on the net was a soft-drink vending machine in a corridor somewhere in a US university hooked up by TCP/IP to the net. Visitors could see what drinks were available, and what was cold or out of stock. Compared to the facilities available on the net today, that seems laughable now.

As you flick through this book you'll find boxes, just like this, at the start of some chapters. They'll tell you what material you'll find on the CD-ROM at the back of the book pertaining to that chapter.

HELEN DANCER

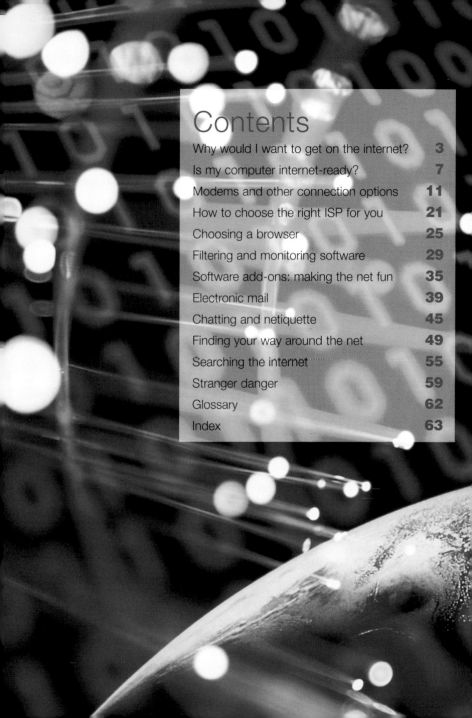

Contents

Why would I want to get on the internet?

Think about the things you have to do today: make a shopping list and brave the supermarket, pay some bills, send a card for a friend's anniversary, buy your aunt a birthday present then wrap it and post it, order a reference book from the library for your next big project – you just *know* they won't have it in stock – and maybe help with the kids' homework.

The good news is that, while you'll still have to cook your own meals and stack your own dishwasher at the end of the day, the internet can help with all the rest of those daily chores, and probably save you heaps of time into the bargain.

The value of the internet increases as more and more people connect to it. Think of the telephone. One telephone by itself is absolutely useless; it becomes useful the minute a second telephone is installed, and more and more useful as further telephones are installed. The internet's the same and, while even five years ago it had a limited appeal, a gee-whiz aura, it has evolved to the point where it is populated by enough companies, services and people to be really useful.

Apart from the must-do things in life, there are stacks of wouldn't-it-be-nice things the net can assist with as well – shopping for rare, out-of-print books and records, trawling the world for obscure collectibles on auction sites, or shopping for luxurious lingerie or the finest golf clubs the world has to offer. If you have a hankering for Moroccan tagine but don't have a recipe book, the net can come to the rescue, with more recipes than you'd ever have time to prepare.

Weird, wonderful and just-plain-useful things to do on the internet

When it comes to what you can find on the internet, you're limited only by your imagination. The following ideas barely scratch the surface.

☐ Throwing a cocktail party? There are endless cocktail sites on the net; often, you can search by the name of the drink or by its ingredients. One site alone has 74 versions of a martini.

☐ Lonely hearts alert! Finding a partner, through a multiplicity of chat rooms, has never been easier – but read Stranger Danger, page 59, before you act on this.

☐ If astrology is your cup of tea, read your daily horoscope on the web.

☐ So languages aren't your forte? The net can help with its many translation and dictionary sites. Translate Arabic into Welsh, Albanian to Spanish or Swahili to English, all at the press of a button.

☐ For the hypochondriac in the family: medical websites can help identify any complaint, from hypoglycaemia to bipolar disorder – but are no replacement for a trip to the doctor!

☐ If you've got a little extra love to give, why not adopt a pet over the net?

☐ For tech-heads, the web has a positive plethora of sites devoted to keeping you up-to-date with the latest toys for grown-ups.

☐ Are you looking to buy real estate? Take a virtual tour of any property that catches your eye – you won't have to leave home to either fall in love, or decide it's a case of renovate or detonate!

In the time it takes to get into your car, drive to the supermarket and find a parking spot, then walk from your car to the front door, you could:

☐ visit a supermarket or specialist food supplier on the net and make an order to be delivered to your front door

☐ go to your virtual bank account on line and check whether your pay has been credited to your account, and then BPay the bills that have been piling up

☐ go to a greeting card site on the net, choose a suitable card and write your own greeting and, if your friend has an e-mail address, e-mail the card

☐ jump from there to a gift-giving service, choose your aunt's present, some appropriate wrapping and a card, write your own message and have the company deliver it to her

☐ go to a search engine and type in a key phrase for that next big project and, at the click of a mouse, have access to all the resources the net has to offer.

Cyberspace is not scary, it's not even hard to get to. Just step this way...

Is my computer internet-ready?

Your computer is waiting impatiently on the desk,
ready to make the leap into cyberspace, but are you
prepared? Try this quick quiz.

Do you have...

A modem, either internal (located inside the system
unit – this is also known as a modem card) or external?
A modem is a device for encoding and decoding the
data you send and receive across the internet. The phone
line, which is the transmission medium, carries waves
in analogue form, and the data on your computer is
stored in digital form; thus the modem must **mo**dulate
and **dem**odulate the data (hence the name) so it can
be carried to the destination and reconfigured, so the
receiving computer can make sense of it. The same
applies in reverse to get information back to you.
Modern modems transmit information at a rate of
56,000 bits per second (56 kilobits per second, or Kbps)
or as fast as the telephone infrastructure can carry it.

A phone line close at hand into which you can
plug your modem? The phone line is your computer's
lifeline to the rest of the world, so if you plan on spending
a lot of time on line, it might be worth considering
putting in a dedicated phone line for your modem
connection, since nobody in the household will be
able to receive or make phone calls while you're on the
net. If you choose one of the more advanced (and more
expensive) connection options (see pages 15-19),
you might be able to reclaim the line for simultaneous
voice traffic and internet surfing, but a modem is a
phone-line hog. If you've opted for a dial-up modem
connection, it's all or nothing.

YOU'LL ALSO NEED...

The other stuff you need,
such as browser software,
an e-mail account, and
the various plug-ins
(software which will make
your experience of the web
easier and more interesting)
are all available once
you get out there into
cyberspace. And to make it
even simpler, we've put
them all on the CD-ROM
that comes with this book.

Modems and other connection options

In order to connect to the internet, you first need a modem, the means by which most home computer users log onto the net.

What is a modem?

A modem, or dial-up connection, is by far the most common method of connecting your home computer to the internet. Modem technology has improved in leaps and bounds since the first readily available models, which offered transmission speeds of just 1200 and then 2400 bits per second. Inevitably, the technology has matured, making modems faster, easier to install and more stable to run. Connection technologies such as USB (Universal Serial Bus) and Firewire, protocols such as Plug and Play, smarter software and faster transmission rates have all contributed to ensure that installing and running a modem is now far from the headache it used to be.

The speed to expect in a modem is 56K (56,000 bits per second). This might also be called a V.90 standard. Ignore the jargon – it's the same device, transmitting at the same speed.

A good quality modem should cost no more than a couple of hundred dollars and, if you're buying a computer too, it's far more cost-effective to include a modem as part of the deal.

OUT WITH THE OLD

If you are replacing an existing modem, it is highly recommended that you remove all the modem software associated with the old modem before you start installing a new one. Follow the instruction manual for the old modem to completely remove all the relevant components, to avoid any chance of unnecessary complications with your new set up.

On the CD-ROM:
■ Up-to-date modem drivers
■ Links to websites detailing fast connection options

HOLD ALL CALLS

If all your communications software is working well, but you're having problems sustaining your internet connection, the culprit could be Call Waiting. The "beep beep" sound that tells you someone's waiting on the line to talk to you is enough interference to break your internet connection. Turn Call Waiting off while you're on the net, but don't forget to enable it once you finish. Or, if it's a dedicated modem line, cancel it entirely; you won't need it.

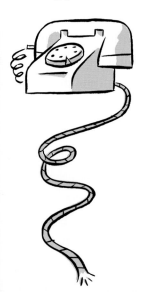

Internal or external?

A modem can be included in your computer purchase either as an internal or external modem. An internal modem is a secondary card attached to an expansion slot in your system case at the time the computer is built. All you can see of an internal modem is the small phone jack into which you plug the phone cable to connect the computer to the phone line. An internal modem card usually also offers fax capabilities, to turn your computer into a de facto fax machine, capable of receiving faxes and of faxing any documents you create.

An external modem is a separate box that sits on the desk or on top of the system unit, and plugs into the computer and the phone line – it is far easier to add an external modem to an existing computer than to add an internal modem.

An external modem will require its own power source, i.e., an extra plug to allow for in your system set up, but it will perform exactly the same data transfer function as a modem card, without the fax capabilities. You can, of course, add fax software to your computer in order to bestow your external modem with fax capabilities. One benefit of an external modem is that it is easy to tell if any communications problems are due to a fault in the modem or somewhere else down the line; you simply check if the lights are flashing (or not, as the case may be) to determine if the modem is at least trying.

An external modem plugs into your computer either as a serial connection or, increasingly commonly, as a USB or Firewire connection, and into the phone socket in the wall.

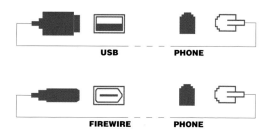

USB   PHONE

FIREWIRE   PHONE

Connecting an external modem

The type of cable connecting the computer and the modem will make small differences to the process of installing it.

For serial connections (older Windows PCs)

If the connection type is a serial cable, start with the computer turned OFF.

1. Plug one end of the cable into the corresponding jack on the back of the modem, and the other end into the COM (i.e., serial) port on your computer; tighten the screws. See diagram below right.

2. Then plug one end of the telephone cable into the modem's phone jack, and the other end into the phone socket in the wall. Most modems have a second phone jack, into which you can plug the telephone so you can use it when the modem's not in use.

3. Plug the power adaptor into the back of the modem, and into the power point and turn it on.

4. Turn your computer on and let it boot up.

5. Put the CD that came with the modem package into the CD-ROM drive. If you're running Windows 95 or 98, it should run automatically, but if it doesn't, click on Start, then Run, and type D:\ into the appropriate box (substitute the letter representing your CD-ROM drive if it's not the D drive), and click the browse button. Look for a file called Set Up or Install; click to run the set-up procedure. Follow the instructions on screen, click Finish to finish set up and return to the main screen. If you're running Windows XP, run the Printers & Other Hardware Wizard you'll find in the Control Panel.

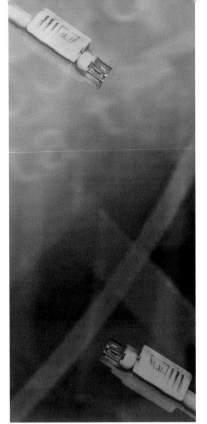

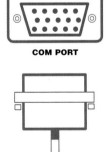

COM PORT

For USB Connections (Windows PCs)

If the connection type is a USB cable, it may not be essential to turn the computer off first.

1. Connect the USB cable to your modem, and one end of the phone cable into the phone jack on the back of the modem and the other into the wall socket. You can also plug the telephone into the other phone jack so you can use it on that line when the modem is not in use.

2. Plug the other end of the USB cable into the USB port of the computer. When you attach the modem, Windows will ask for the driver software.

3. Put the CD in the CD-ROM drive; follow the Add New Hardware Wizard instructions on screen, which will be different depending on your Windows version, clicking on the option to use your own CD when prompted to tell the computer where the driver is found.

4. Click Finish at the end to complete the installation process.

For USB Connections (iMacs)

1. Close down all applications except Finder.

2. Insert the modem's software CD in the CD-ROM drive.

3. When the CD icon appears on your screen, double-click on it and then on Installer. Click on the driver installation button. This will install the drivers you need from the CD.

4. Click Yes to continue the installation, but don't restart your computer as prompted until you have connected the modem to it.

5. Connect the USB cable to your modem, and one end of the phone cable into the jack on the back of your modem and the other into the wall socket. You can also plug the telephone into the other phone jack so you can use it on that line when the modem is not in use.

6. Plug the other end of the USB cable into the USB port of your computer. Warning: For iMac users, the plug looks very much the same as the one for your keyboard. Make sure you don't plug your modem cable into your keyboard port.

7. Now Click Restart to finish the installation process.

8. To make the modem you've just installed the default modem for your computer, click on Open Modem Control Panel once the computer has restarted and select USB from the Connect via menu. Select the modem type. And you're done.

What other connection options exist?

A modem connection is fine for the average internet user, for those who don't spend all day every day on line, and whose use of the net doesn't include too many large files, such as sound or video. But for those who plan on using the net for acquiring lots of MP3 files, or for watching, downloading or sending lots of graphics and video files, then there are faster (albeit more expensive) options. Apart from the one-off cost of the modem, a dial-up connection entails signing up with an ISP, which shouldn't cost more than $30/month for an average domestic usage plan, and the cost of the phone calls.

Cable internet

Cable internet runs on the same infrastructure that brings pay-TV into your home, and offers an internet connection that is roughly nine times faster than a dial-up modem connection (512Kbps). It uses dedicated hybrid fibre-coaxial cable, rather than simply plugging into the standard phone line the way a modem does. To run cable internet you will need a cable modem, different from a standard modem, and more expensive, and the installation team will also need to fit your computer with an Ethernet (network) card. For this investment, you then have a connection which is always "on", rather than having to turn on and dial up every time you want to get on the net. Cable internet services transfer data faster downstream, i.e., to your home, than upstream, i.e., from your computer back into cyberspace, since most of us use the internet to consume information we find there, rather than publishing material to it. So while the download speed is around 512Kbps, the upload speed is about 128Kbps – still fast enough to dramatically improve your experience on the net.

One of the upsides of cable is that you get double the functionality from the same infrastructure – pay-TV and internet. Cable companies offer attractive packages for customers who want to take advantage of multiple services,

so adding internet access to an existing pay-TV account might be quite cost effective. The cost of installing cable to run a net connection, rather than adding it to an existing pay-TV contract, includes a one-off installation fee (which can stretch into the hundreds of dollars) and monthly fees of around $50 for a medium-fast service with an average download allowance to more like $75/month for a faster service and higher download thresholds. Since the data flows faster in one direction than the other, the speed of the connection is expressed in terms of both – e.g., 256/64, or 256Kbps download and 64Kbps upload.

Using cable, however, can get a bit crowded. The cable infrastructure is shared between a fixed number of people, each of whom get a diminishing share as more people connect to the same sector; thus, the speed of your cable connection depends on how many other people in your area are tuned in at the same time. And if the neighbour is being a bandwidth hog, i.e., downloading lots of files, then you'll get less space (bandwidth) to do the things you want to do, so you'll find them taking longer. Cable providers have been known to warn users whose downloads are out of proportion, and to restrict or terminate repeat offenders.

To set up a cable connection, your computer must be able to allocate some of its resources to running the connection. Check the following table for the minimum specifications of a computer on which you can run a cable internet connection.

MINIMUM SPECIFICATIONS FOR RUNNING CABLE INTERNET

PC	MACINTOSH
Pentium Processor	Power PC
Win 95, 98 or XP, or Win NT4	OS 8 with Open Transport
16 M RAM (for Windows 95/98/XP)	TCP/IP v1.1 or later
24 M RAM (for Windows NT4)	24 M RAM
Free ISA or PCI slot (for Ethernet card)	Ethernet interface
SVGA display 800x600x256 colours	800x600x256 colour display
CD-ROM drive, sound card and speakers	CD-ROM drive, sound card and speakers

ISDN

ISDN (Integrated Services Digital Network) is a faster transmission technology using the phone infrastructure, but the phone lines must be digital.

The benefit of ISDN over a standard modem connection is that it offers two lines (rather than one) over standard copper wire (the phone infrastructure), both of which can transmit data at around 64Kbps, or twice as fast as a standard modem. With ISDN it's also possible to make and receive phone calls, or send or receive faxes at the same time as you're connected to the internet, because the technology uses the wires in a shared capacity.

One of the main reasons that companies installed ISDN when it was first released was this shared capacity; they could add internet capability to existing phone lines rather than installing more connections as dedicated lines. And because the line is a digital, rather than analogue one, the clarity of transmission of data should be better.

The benefits for the home user are pretty much the same – faster access times, less time waiting for a download to finish, and an efficient internet surfing experience, with the advantage of being able to use the same line for phone calls.

One of the downsides is the cost of the connection; even local calls may be charged on a timed, rather than flat-rate basis. Be sure to check the fine print of the fees that apply.

ISDN has the advantage over other faster connection options of being more widely available. Most people living within reasonable distance of an exchange (say between 4.5km and 7km), can opt for ISDN as long as the exchange has been upgraded to digital lines. Its other advantage over cable is that your connection is entirely your own, and is not shared with the neighbours.

Rates for ISDN vary according to usage, so consider your needs carefully before signing up. For example, three hours a month could cost an average of $3/hour, with extra hours charged at even higher rates, whereas a 70-hours-a-month plan might work out at a much more attractive $1/hour, with a lower cost for additional hours into the bargain.

HOW FAST IS FAST?

To put the speeds of the available options in context, consider this: downloading a nine megabyte file using a modem dial-up connection at the maximum speed possible, 56Kbps, would take roughly 25 minutes. To download the same file over an ISDN line at 128Kbps would take around 10 minutes. And over an ADSL connection, the same file, travelling at 1.5 megabits per second (or 1500Kbps), would take around 48 seconds.

How to choose the right ISP for you

Choosing the right ISP is a matter of careful research; it is also important that you realistically assess how much time you are going to spend on line each month to make the most cost-effective decision.

Plan your plan

Most service providers these days offer packages based on a fixed (or sometimes unlimited) number of hours' access, rather than an access fee and hours charged on top.

With fixed-hour packages, any extra hours spent on line are charged at a higher rate; if you're on the net consistently longer than first planned, you could blow your budget.

As with any bulk-buy proposition, the more hours you pay for, the cheaper the per-hour rate is likely to be. However, you don't want to pay for time you're not using. Be aware that most ISPs won't let you roll over the unused hours into the following month, so you either use it or lose it.

If you are unsure of the amount of time you will use, find a plan that doesn't lock you in, and avoid anything long term. It may be worth choosing a more flexible plan for the first few months, even at a higher rate, to help you gain an idea of your average monthly usage; you can then use this knowledge to find the deal that best suits your needs.

Local call access

It's important to make sure that the ISP you choose has a local-call dial-up number, especially if you don't reside in a capital city. Remember that when you connect to the internet you pay the phone company for the phone call, the ISP for the access, and then the rate per hour, unless you choose some sort of access plus hours package.

If the phone call you make to connect to your ISP is an untimed local call, then it just represents a small fixed cost per internet visit. But if you're paying STD (long distance) rates on the phone call every time you connect, this will quickly escalate your internet access bill to something quite out of proportion to the benefit of being on line. And if you have teenagers who love to chat, surf or play multi-user on-line games, the bills can rack up faster than you can say cyberheadache.

Read the fine print

As with anything in life, a deal that seems like a bargain may not be as good as it looks when you dig a little deeper. For example, some connection packages may tie you to one access point, which may be fine if you only ever want to use your account from your home computer. But if you're on the road and want to check your e-mail, make a quick net search or pay a bill from your on-line bank account, you won't have the luxury of dialling that company's local POP (Point of Presence), and may have to dial long-distance back to the POP you signed up with. This may be irritating, but it's probably not that big a deal; just bear it in mind.

Internet access also falls squarely into the category of no-such-thing-as-a-free-lunch. If a company offers you "free" access, it's probably a good idea to ask yourself what the catch is. Sometimes, free access is offered in return for providing information about yourself, which the access provider then sells to other companies who would like to market their products at you.

If you don't mind being bombarded with e-mails from people you've never heard of and probably don't want to buy from, or flooded with offers from every man and his cyberdog, in return for cost-free access, then go ahead. There's nothing intrinsically wrong with these services, it's just a matter of being aware of the conditions that apply. Every ISP should offer a Privacy Policy that spells out how it plans on using the information you give about yourself when you sign up. If a company doesn't declare its privacy policy up front, you should think twice about signing up. If you feel that you've suffered a breach of the privacy policy then you can complain to the Telecommunications Industry Ombudsman.

Finally, read the fine print on the contract before you sign. You might find that you're locked into a lengthy period of time, say 12 or 18 months, and that terminating the account means you have to pay out the length of the contract. Again, there's nothing intrinsically wrong with such an arrangement, if you can see that far into the future and are happy that the access package you're committing to will be sufficient for your needs that far into the future. Understand, though, that once you sign you're stuck with it, and if you decide you've made a mistake, it could turn out to be a costly one.

Other Mac browsers

iCab

A Mac-only browser from German software house iCab Company, iCab is a no-nonsense, no-frills browser that offers useful features, such as a cookie filter, and many of the other standard browser attributes. It is commercially available, or can be downloaded from http://www.icab.de/.

Mac and Windows browsers

Opera

This shareware browser is available not only for Mac, but also for Windows, and a range of lesser known operating systems such as BeOS, Linux, OS/2 and EPOC. It needs less in the way of resources and provides a good range of browser functions. You can download the browser from www.opera.com, but remember, it's shareware – if you like it, you really ought to pay for it ($US10).

Mozilla

Mozilla is a browser built on a modular framework, i.e., to some extent you take the bits you want and leave the rest, and offers optional mail and news tools. Read about Mozilla at http://www.mozilla.org, but be aware that if you download and use this browser, it's open source. This means that people are working on it all the time – it's a work in progress. On top of that, there's no product support available, so be prepared to fly solo.

There is also a version for the Linux operating system.

Browsers for older Windows systems

If you're running an old Windows version on a second-hand PC, it probably won't have the grunt to run new browsers. There's not much you can do, bar trying an older copy of Navigator or IE if you can find one, or try Opera.

Opera

Opera's Windows version will work on a 386SX running Windows 3.1 and requires only 8M of RAM. It provides compatibility with most web pages, i.e., the technology incorporated in it can deal with more modern technologies used in website design, and can also deal with point to point security issues. Opera is also available in a Windows 95/NT version. It is shareware, so you can download and try it, but if you plan to keep on using it, send that cheque!

Browsers for modern Windows systems

While no other products offer feature sets and ease-of-use comparable to either of the main commercial browsers – and, what's more, both are free! – if you have your heart set on getting out of the mainstream, try these alternatives.

Opera

This browser uses far less in the way of system resources, and offers a large cross section of the functions you might expect from the major brands. Go to www.opera.com to download.

Neoplanet

Not technically a browser, NeoPlanet is an add-on to Internet Explorer designed to make browsing easier, especially for beginners. It's very lightweight (less than 4M) and easy to download (http://www.neoplanet.com). NeoPlanet is individualistic, and includes a gallery of "skins" to make your browser look anything but ordinary. It also organises content into useful channels, to make it easier to find what you're looking for.

your child safe-surfing practices is essential, rather than relying on a software solution alone.

It's not too dissimilar from teaching your child not to talk to strangers. It's also important to remind them that, because the people we chat with on the internet are faceless, we all have to work a lot harder to make sure they are who they say they are, and be careful about telling them anything personal. Questions such as: "Where do you live?", "What's your phone number?", "Are Mummy and Daddy at home?" and "What's Mummy's credit card number?" should set off warning bells in a child's mind. Remind your child that they got into the chat room or website at the click of a mouse and can get out just as easily. There's no need to feel embarrassed about not answering a question – just leave.

Bigger brother to the rescue

Governments around the world are struggling with the need to protect their citizens from harm without infringing on their civil liberties, in respect to access to information.

In Australia, efforts to control access to inappropriate material and protect children from potential danger include the passing of legislation making the ISP responsible for providing a filtering and monitoring solution for home users, or at least asking the home user if they want this kind of solution.

When you sign up with an ISP you have the option of declining to have it provide you any kind of filtering solution, or accepting it in one of two ways. If you decline, that puts the onus back on you to monitor your children's access to the internet – you can't then complain to the Australian Broadcasting Authority (ABA) if the kids find something horrible while your back was turned.

If you accept, you can choose to have the ISP provide you with a package that you install on your own desktop and customise to suit your family's needs, or you can elect for the ISP to provide you with a server-based filtering system, i.e., filter from its end, rather than from yours, a list of sites and subject matter that it, not you, decides is inappropriate for you and your family. A server-based filtering system is a good alternative if you're reluctant to customise your own filtering package, or feel that your kids are a little mischievous and might try to override the system (every parent's fear is that the kids know more about the rotten machine than they do, right?). This will ultimately be the most draconian and restrictive option because the ISP is put in the difficult position of trying to please all of the people all of the time.

Looking for the perfect filtering and monitoring software

There's no such thing as perfect, because the internet is a moveable feast, and a site that finds it is being blocked by name can easily change its name, and so the chase becomes an endless battle between filtering software developer and website developer. No one product can hope to be all things to all people either, because we all have such different notions about what's acceptable and what's not.

What you can do, however, is look at the products on the market against a checklist of how well they implement the various features that you consider important.

Server or client?

Do you want a server side solution or a client-based package? A server side solution is one that monitors the internet from somewhere outside your home and, as with the ISP solution explained above, decides on which material could be deemed inappropriate and then blocks it. This is usually a subscription service for which you pay a monthly fee, rather than a one-off purchase or yearly update price. A client, or desktop-based, solution can be distributed as a download direct from the developer or in a shrink-wrapped box of software that you buy, take home, load up and configure to suit your own family's values. When you buy a shrink-wrapped or downloaded product, however, check whether you're buying a lifetime usage or a product that needs to be updated annually for a fee.

FILTER ON DEMAND

Choose a product that filters on demand, according to established keywords, rather than simply checking any site about to be visited against a database of restricted sites. Sites come and go, and change their guise in the space of hours, so any database is only going to stay up to date while it is being created, which will render any inflexible package less than efficient long term.

To block or not to block?

The issue of blocking is two-edged because of the difficulty of creating software that is capable of blocking inappropriate material according to keywords, without also inadvertently screening out related but acceptable material. Software is based on rules, not sensibilities, so when it finds a site about breast cancer, for example, it can't distinguish the positive content from, say, a less altruistic site featuring the same body parts, and so the software will block both sites. A product's ability to be customised into many layers of content rather than just screening according to broad keywords like Sex, Drugs, Violence, and so on, is a good idea.

New-fangled technology that filters sites not only based on the words employed in the metatags or the site name, but also on the amount of skin tone on any given page, goes a long way to overcoming the sneaky practice of calling a lascivious site something perfectly innocent, like www.littlegreenfrog.com, but it is still in early development stages and not available for home users.

Restrict and permit

Some products overcome the blanket ban problem by incorporating a special restrict and permit filter which will restrict broad categories such as sex, but specifically allow access to certain sites within it (identified by name), such as sex education and health issues sites, which you might consider valuable resources for your children.

Site logging

If you want to know where your children have been surfing, to keep track of whether they are abiding by the rules you've set, look for a product that will provide you with a log of where they went on any internet session, and enable you to identify any that fall outside the agreed acceptable zone.

Time control

As with anything, computer time can turn into too much of a good thing. Some products on the market will allow you to set time controls to encourage your little mouse potatoes to experience life beyond the screen. After an agreed amount of time, the computer will simply tell the user that enough is enough, and log off.

INTERNET FILTERING AND MONITORING PRODUCTS

The following list is intended as a guide and not as a recommendation or endorsement of any particular product. Another option is to activate the Family Filter option available on Alta Vista's search engine http://www.altavista.com (or your country's local version) to filter material found in internet searches.

PRODUCT	COMPANY
Internet Filtering Manager	N2H2

http://www.n2h2.com/solutions/home/index.html

Bounce	Bounce

http://www.kidswebbrowser.com/entry.html?why bounce.html

CyberPatrol	SurfControl

http://www.surfcontrol.com/products/cyberpatrol_for_home/product_overview/index.html

CyberSnoop	Pearl Software

http://www.pearlsoftware.com/home/index.html

Cybersitter 2000	Solid Oak Software

http://www.cybersitter.com/

Internet Guard Dog	McAfee

http://mcafeestore.beyond.com/Category/0,1257,3-18-1148,00.html

Norton Internet Security 2001	Symantec

http://www.symantec.com/

NetNanny	Net Nanny

http://www.netnanny.com

KidSafe	Apple

http://kidsafe.apple.com/

Software add-ons: making the net fun

There is a range of useful small software programs, known as add-ons or plug-ins, that have been designed to make your use of the net more fun, by adding the capability for your machine to read the music, video and complex documents that sites have to offer.

Modern site design uses complex technology to present an all-singing all-dancing face to the world. Incorporating video and stereo music, large animated graphics and complex documents makes the site more interesting to look at but relies on every receiving computer having the matching components. Usually, this kind of technology is designed in two parts: a creation tool, and a reader or receiver. The software developer will derive revenue from selling the content creation or player part to companies wanting to incorporate sound and video on their website, and provide them to the reader or receiver free of charge so that as many people as possible can use it to make the most of these multimedia sites.

And don't worry if you have one type of media player already on your system and a website demands a different kind – they are all designed to be incredibly compact and not at all resource hungry, so you can have multiple players on your system without causing a load. Most likely, however, the site will pick up on whichever player you have installed and decide it can work with that one. So you're ready for any eventuality!

MULTIMEDIA PLAYERS

Most of the products on the following pages are designed to make viewing of video files and listening to audio files, created by a website's developer, faster and more fluid, or to play, store and record music as MP3 files. Because audio and video files are typically large, incorporating a lot of data, they either take a long time to get from the website's server to your desktop or look or sound jerky while being transmitted. Media players use compression technology to make the transition and replay as smooth as possible.

On the CD-ROM:
■ Media players, Adobe Acrobat, Macromedia Flash, Shockwave, QuickTime

Where can I get these add-ons?

There are three ways you can acquire these useful software products. The most common is when you try and visit a site that uses that particular technology; if your computer doesn't have the matching reader components installed, the site will suggest you download the reader software then and there. Alternatively, go to the software developer's own website and download the add-on directly. There, you might find more sophisticated versions available at a price; you can decide whether you want the basic, usually free model or the fancy version at a cost. Usually, these software developers are American, so be prepared to assess the value of the software in $US rather than local currency. The third, and far simplest way of acquiring these add-ons is by using the trial versions of these products on the CD you'll find at the back of this book.

Useful internet add-ons

Adobe Acrobat Reader

From Adobe (http://www.adobe.com), Acrobat Reader is the free reader version of Adobe's document management software, Acrobat. Complex, legal and write-protected documents are created in Acrobat to make them easier to store and send, and to read in the format the creator intended; it protects them from being edited or otherwise compromised either on the site, in transit or by the reader.

Macromedia Flash Player

This is a reader for animated and entertainment-type content created on a website in Macromedia Flash.
http://www.macromedia.com/software/flash/download/

Macromedia Shockwave Player

This is a reader for applications created using Shockwave. Such applications are typically those that use multimedia, such as games, or invite a great deal of interactivity, such as chat applications. http://www.macromedia.com/software/shockwaveplayer/download/

QuickTime Player

Originally created by Apple for the Mac platform, QuickTime has spread to the Windows world as well, and is now near ubiquitous as a tool for creating and playing audio and video files. QuickTime is famous as the enabling technology that allowed millions of net users to download the sneak preview trailer from the Star Wars movie *The Phantom Menace*. Download the QuickTime Player from http://www.apple.com/quicktime/download/.

RealAudio/RealPlayer

A pioneering internet audio player from RealNetworks, RealAudio enabled users to listen to music in real time or tune in to one of the thousands of internet radio stations. The audio player has since been incorporated into RealPlayer, which includes high fidelity video playing as well. Download RealPlayer from http://www.real.com/player/index.html?src=noref, rnhmpg_020701,rnhmtn,prdctmn_02210.

There are two versions available – a basic, free player and a more upmarket version for which RealNetworks charges a fee.

RealJukebox

This turns your computer into a MP3 recording, storing and playing machine. Download RealJukebox from http://www.real. com/jukebox/index.html?src=noref,rnhmpg _020701,rnhmtn,prdctmn_022101. Again, there's a basic, free Jukebox and a fancier one for a price.

Windows Media Player

Microsoft's freely available audio and video player can be found at http://www.microsoft.com/ windows/windowsmedia/en/default.asp

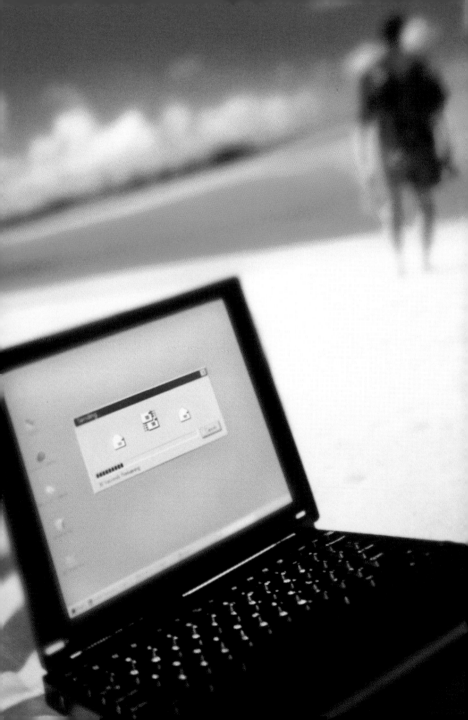

Electronic mail

E-mail is electronic mail, letters, electronic postcards and other communications that you write on your computer and send to other e-mail addresses anywhere in the world.

To send and receive e-mail, from an account to be used mostly at home, you'll need: a computer with modem so you can access the internet; an e-mail address (which you'll invariably get from your ISP); and an account with an ISP.

Your address

An e-mail address has three parts: your name, the domain name of the provider who hosts your e-mail, and a signifier of what sort of domain it is, for example, janesmith@thebestisp.com.

The janesmith part identifies you, the @ symbol means at, the name of the company (the domain where your e-mail lives) is next, and what sort of domain it is, i.e., a company or commercial domain (.com), a non-profit domain (.org), an educational domain (.edu) or a government domain (.gov).

If you want to run a small business, you can register your own name or business name as a domain on the internet, as in janesmith@flowerbaskets.com, but otherwise the domain name of the service provider will be the one you're stuck with.

On the CD-ROM:
- A range of free web-based e-mail packages
- Spam filters

CAN THE SPAM

One distressing downside to signing up for free e-mail is the amount of junk e-mail you'll get, for services you'll probably never need, from bogus university diplomas, lose weight campaigns and lots and lots of net sex, lewd pictures and more. Indiscriminately sent junk e-mail is popularly known as Spam.

Most e-mail packages offer a Block Sender option, to help you filter out repeat e-mails from services that bother or offend. You can't stop them gaining access to your address, but you can prevent them from repeatedly hassling you. Unfortunately, spammers often change their address to duck the Block option, so you'll need to be vigilant, and knock them on the head as soon as they appear in another guise. Sending them a reply, asking them not to e-mail you, is invariably pointless.

What kind of e-mail address do I need?

If you don't have your own computer and therefore don't have an ISP account, but still want to use e-mail, say, if you're planning on travelling and want to keep in touch with the folks back home, you can sign up for a free web-based e-mail address. Web-based e-mail is exactly that – e-mail that lives on a web server, stored in cyberspace and accessible from wherever on the planet you are when you want to read it. You can access it from any computer with an up-to-date browser, whether it's at an internet cafe or a public library, or the home of someone you meet along the way. The computer needn't have any special receiving software on it; you simply have to remember your user name and password to access your own mailbox.

Since you don't pay a fee for such an e-mail account, the revenue has to come from somewhere – the e-mail provider probably survives on advertising revenue, so you're likely to be subjected to a lot of ads, either that or the company will on-sell the data you've given about yourself. You decide whether the easy cost-free access is worth the volume of junk mail.

The advantages of web-based e-mail are the fact that it's free and accessible from anywhere. The downside is that, since your e-mail is stored on the provider's web servers along with everyone else's, it piles up fast, so pretty soon the provider will start clearing out your old messages, or warning that if you don't clear out your mailbox it will do the job for you.

The e-mail address you'll get with your ISP account is called a POP-based e-mail address, meaning it's stored on a server at the ISP's Point Of Presence (i.e., the point you've signed up). With this kind of system, your messages are stored on the provider's server until you are ready to read them, then downloaded to your own computer. One of the main benefits of POP mail accounts is that you can spend time creating messages off-line and connect just to receive and send mail, rather than be connected the whole time you are writing, sending and receiving mail. You can also re-read old messages without having to connect to the net because, once downloaded, they are stored on your computer's own hard drive. The downside of POP-based e-mail used to be that you could not access it from just anywhere, because the computer on which you received it had to have the right software but, increasingly, POP-based e-mail can be read from any computer with a browser, though if you're not at home you won't want to leave copies of your private correspondence on other people's computers. You'll also be a target for on-site advertising banners, and a fair amount of marketing e-mail directed to your in-box.

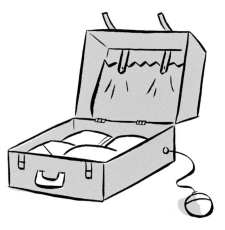

Creating and sending e-mail

While it's fair to say all e-mail packages have their idiosyncrasies, it's also true that they have more in common than not.

Creating and sending e-mail is a very simple affair; start by launching the e-mail package you have and clicking on Create Memo (or Create Message or New Memo or New Mail). That will give you a screen with fields such as To:, Cc:, Bcc:, Subject: and the message space. Now, simply type the e-mail address of the person (or multiple addresses to send the same e-mail to lots of people at once) in the To: bar.

Adding other addresses in the Cc: bar will allow the original addressees to see that the other person has been copied in on the message. Putting names in the Bcc: bar sends a copy of the message to other people but hides the fact from the original addressee.

When you have written your message in the message space, simply click Send, or Send and Save If you want to save a copy of your message for future reference.

If you want to organise your messages into, say, work correspondence and family correspondence, you can create folders, name them appropriately, and file both sent and received mail into these folders.

If you have a message that's not quite ready to send, you can choose to Save as Draft, and keep it to work on some other time.

Receiving and reading e-mail

When you dial up to send and receive mail from a POP-based mail account, there will usually be a button called something like Send and Receive Mail. Clicking on this button will initiate the process, your computer will query the mail server, which will then "deliver" all the mail that has been waiting for you since you last checked and upload any messages you have created on your own machine. Once it has finished, you can either disconnect and read your downloaded e-mails at your leisure, or read them

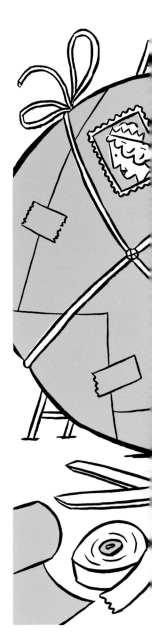

quickly and respond straightaway. Once you have created a response and clicked on the Send button, click on Send and Receive again to upload your response to the mail server and send it on its way. Don't forget to disconnect from your ISP when you have finished sending and receiving e-mail; time is money!

Adding attachments to e-mails

E-mail is a wonderful vehicle for sending whole documents, photos of the kids, even animated images, on the proviso that you can condense them to make them easy to send and receive. There's something really irritating about waiting for a big fat e-mail to download. Macs use Stuffit!, and Windows uses WinZip to compress large files. Saving photos as jpeg files also makes them quite send-friendly.

Once you have your attachment in fit shape to travel, simply create a memo and, in the message space, click Attach Document (or Make Attachment, or the Insert menu then click again on File Attachment), and find the folder on the hard drive in which the document lives, and click on it to attach a copy to the e-mail. You'll see an icon representing that document in the message space of the e-mail you're creating. Then press Send and Save in the same way as normal, and your picture or document is on its way.

Change your details

If you've changed your name since you set up your e-mail account, or want to add an extra name to it – from Ted Cooper, say, to Ted and Alice Cooper, if two people want to share an e-mail address, you can do this in the user name and details section of your e-mail package. In Outlook Express, for example, go to the Tools menu and choose Accounts and, if you have more than one account, choose the one you want to change (most people will have only one). Click on that account, and then click Properties, which should bring up a field marked User Information, including a Name field. The name that appears on your outgoing messages is displayed there, so change it to whatever name(s) you want your messages to display.

Chatting and netiquette

Anyone for a chat?

Chatting is one step more immediate than e-mail – real time conversational exchanges between two or more people, using their keyboards rather than their voices.

Unlike e-mail, which can be sent and picked up at the convenience of either party, chatters need to be on the internet at the same time, so you can either go to a chat room and chat to whoever happens to be there, or arrange to be on line at the same time as the person you want to talk to. When you meet in a chat room and start to chat, the conversation you have is visible to everyone else in the room, so two people who meet and want to have a conversation alone can elect to "go private". When you go into the world of chat, it's advisable to select yourself a nickname, or chatting identity (also called a handle), rather than using your real name.

Chat rooms are public spaces set up to cater to people with common interests; chat forums, on the other hand, are scheduled events hosted by a website, and usually include a celebrity or expert in a certain field. These forums are advertised in advance so people interested in participating know when to log in, either to read what the expert has to say, or join in by adding comments or asking questions. There's no law that says you have to speak up, however – you can visit a chat forum just to see what's going on. Such forums are generally monitored, and the moderator has the right to exclude people who use foul language or are otherwise disruptive. If you miss a chat forum, don't despair, there's usually a transcript of the entire conversation saved somewhere on the site.

WARNING

It is important to be wary of giving out information about yourself to people you meet in a chat room. Because of the faceless nature of the internet, the people you meet in cyberspace may not necessarily be who they say they are, and may not have intentions as pure as your own. Never tell someone in a chat room your real name, your home address or your phone number, or anything personal about yourself.

Chat software, or instant messaging software, facilitates keyboard conversations between two people, just like fast e-mail. It typically looks like a split screen; you see the words you type in one half of the screen, and the other person's replies in the other half. Depending on the speed of your connection, you should be able to see the other person's replies as fast as they can type. Unlike e-mail, where the receiver and sender can use different packages, chatters must use the same software in order to communicate.

Once you sign up with an instant messaging service, you'll get a log-in identifier. Send this to other people you want to be able to chat with, and when they type in your identifier they'll be able to see if you're on line and available to chat. Having such an identifier stops you from being hassled by people you don't know, because nobody will know how to get in touch with you unless you tell them.

Netiquette: minding your cybermanners

Netiquette is the art of etiquette on the internet, a largely unwritten and constantly evolving code of manners. As a newbie, it's best to learn by observing and, when in doubt, say nothing. Netizens can be harsh on what they see as breaches, albeit unintentional ones, of net conventions.

The most common way of unintentionally offending is by SPEAKING IN UPPER CASE. This equates to shouting in the real world and, in the same way you'd be taken aback by someone you hardly knew shouting at you for no reason, using capital letters will provoke the same response. Curb that Caps Lock key and stay out of trouble!

If you shout or act in an otherwise unacceptable way in a chat room, you can expect to be flamed. Flaming is abuse, and can actually consist of expletives or &^%$# keys. Either way, keep your cool and don't respond. Such people are hotheads; the flame is designed to humiliate rather than constructively teach better cyber behaviour. If you've embarrassed yourself, simply leave and come back later, when hopefully you'll find more civil people to talk to.

Chat acronyms

To speed up the conversation and compensate for the sort of expression that only a voice can give, chatters use a lot of e-mail shorthand. Chat acronyms which describe emotions are generally enclosed in <> symbols, as in <BG> (Big Grin), whereas phrases such as TTYL8R (Talk To You Later) are not. Read on for some commonly used chat acronyms:

ADN Any Day Now
AFAIK As Far As I Know
AFK Away From Keyboard
A/S/L? Age/Sex/Location?
B4N Bye for Now
BAK Back At the Keyboard
BBIAB Be Back In A Bit
BBL Be Back Later
BEG Big Evil Grin
(also <BG> Big Grin,
<G> Grin, <EG> Evil Grin,
and <VBG> Very Big Grin)
BFD Big Deal (well, you
get the idea)
BFN Bye For Now
BIOYIOP Blow It Out
Your I/O Port
BTA But Then Again
BTW By The Way
BWTHDIK? But What
The Heck Do I Know?
CUL8R See you later
CYO See You On-line
DBA Doing Business As
DIKU? Do I Know you?
DQMOT Don't Quote
Me On This
EMFBI Excuse Me
For Butting In
EOM End Of Message
EOT End Of Thread
(i.e., of the discussion)
ETLA Extended Three
Letter Acronym
F2F Face to Face
FAQ Frequently Asked
Question
FLA Four Letter Acronym
FMTYEWTK Far More Than
You Ever Wanted To Know
FOAD (Go away) And Die
(a mean-spirited flame)
FOMCL Falling Off My
Chair Laughing

FUD Fear Uncertainty
and Doubt
FWIW For What It's Worth
GA Go Ahead
GAL Get A Life
GD&R Grinning, Ducking
and Running
GIWIST Gee, I Wish
I'd Said That
GMTA Great Minds
Think Alike
HAND Have A Nice Day
HTH Hope That Helps
IAC In Any Case
IANAL I Am Not A
Lawyer (but...)
IHA I Hate Acronyms
IIRC If I Recall Correctly
ILU or ILY I Love You
IMHO In My Humble
Opinion (also IMNSHO,
i.e., In My Not So Humble
Opinion or just IMO)
IOW In Other Words
IRL In Real Life
IYSWIM If You See
What I Mean
JIC Just In Case
KOTC Kiss On The Cheek
KWIM? Know What I Mean?
LOL Laugh Out Loud (also
GOL, Giggling Out Loud)
LTM Laugh To Myself
LTNS Long Time No See
LULAB Love you Like
A Brother (or LULAS –
Love you Like A Sister)
MOSS Member Of the Same
Sex (or MOTOS – Member
Of The Opposite Sex)
MUSM Miss you So Much
NFW! No Way!
NRN No Response
Necessary

OIC Oh, I see
OTOH On The Other Hand
OTTOMH Off The Top
Of My Head
PDA Public Display
of Affection
PITA Pain In The Ass, (also
URAPITA – you are a...)
PMFJIB Pardon Me For
Jumping In But
::POOF:: Leaving the room
PU! That stinks!
ROFL Rolling On the
Floor Laughing (ROFLMBO
– ... My Butt Off)
RSN Real Soon Now
SO Significant Other
SOMY? Sick Of Me Yet?
SWAG Stupid Wild Ass Guess
TAFN That's All For Now
TGIF Thank God It's Friday
THX or TX Thanks
TIA Thanks In Advance
TLA Three Letter Acronym
TLK2UL8R Talk to you Later
(also TTYL)
TMI Too Much Information
TPTB The Powers That Be
TTFN Ta Ta For Now
TTT (I) Thought That Too
UW You're Welcome
WDALYIC Who Died And
Left You In Charge?
WFM Works For Me
WIBNI Wouldn't It Be Nice If
WT? What The... ?
WTG Way To Go!
WTGP? Want To Go Private?
WU? What's Up?
WUF? Where are you From?
WYSIWYG What You See
Is What You Get
YGBSM Rude form of
you must be joking

Customising your home page

To change your default page in Internet Explorer, select Tools, then Internet Options, then General. The first bar in this screen has details about your home page, and the URL (Universal Resource Locator – or address) of the page that's currently set as your default home page. Simply type in the URL of the page you'd like to have as your default page and click Use Default, then OK. When you go back to the screen it will still be at the old address, but clicking on the Home button on your toolbar will take you to your new default home page.

To change your default page in Netscape, click on Edit, then choose Preferences from the drop-down menu, then highlight the address in the box marked Home Page and overtype the URL of your preferred home page; click on OK to apply your change.

One-click wonder

Getting around the net is easy, but forget the double click way of doing things you have learned for using applications – the internet is a one-click medium. Clicking twice will only make the browser call the page twice; this takes longer and is likely to confuse your computer, which could then crash. If your computer seems "stuck" and nothing's happening on-screen, just go and put the kettle on. Be patient, it will sort itself out; remember for next time to only click once!

Hyperlinks and addresses

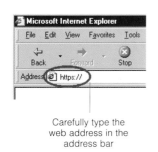

Carefully type the web address in the address bar

Web pages that are relevant to the site you are visiting are called hyperlinks, and are signified by underlined words, or by any element (it might be a picture) that changes the cursor arrow to a pointing hand when it passes over that element. To follow the link, take the cursor to that word, phrase or picture and click once. To go back to the page you came from, click the Back button on the left side of the toolbar.

To go to an entirely new page, go to the Address bar. Type the exact URL (the web address) in the bar carefully – do not omit any punctuation – and click on the Go button.

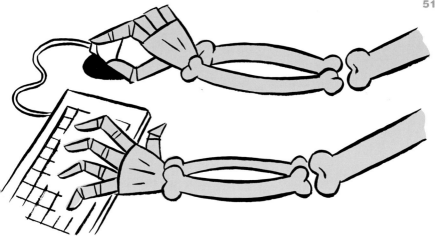

Anatomy of a web address

A web address is made up of the following parts:

http:// This is the instruction from the browser that the information you're asking for is stored on a web server somewhere.

The slightly different prefix https:// means that the server is a secure one and that the site takes responsibility for the security of your confidential information, such as credit card details. This is key to deciding whether you're going to do business with someone over the net. Banks, financial institutions, insurance companies and better retailers all do business on secure servers, so check the security credentials of the site before you impart your credit card number!

Another indicator that a web site is a secure one is that there will be a little padlock in the bottom right-hand corner of the screen.

www. Simply means it's on the World Wide Web, i.e., on a server that's using the protocol HTTP rather than a server that's not.

thecompanyname This appears in lower case, with no spaces between words.

.com The suffix signifies what kind of organisation you're dealing with, e.g., .com is a commercial entity. Others include .org (not for profit organisations), .edu (educational domains), .net (technical organisations, such as ISPs) and .gov (government departments).

.au Sometimes there's a geographic identifier that signifies in which country the website is located – .au for Australia, .nz for New Zealand, .sg for Singapore, and so on. Just to be confusing, however, US websites, as well as domain names registered in the US but located elsewhere, all end in .com, so just because a web address doesn't have a different geographic signifier doesn't automatically make it an American company.

Error

Sometimes when you try a web address either by clicking on a link or typing in a URL, all you'll get is this page:

Problem Report	The system detected an **Unresolved Host Name** while attempting to retrieve the URL: **http://www.bbc/**.
Message ID	UNRESOLVED_HOSTNAME
Problem Description	DNS resolution failure encountered for the host 'www.bbc'.
Possible Problem Cause	The host entered has a mistake, or the requested Web site is temporarily unavailable in DNS.
Possible Solution	Examine or correct any mistakes, or try again at a later time.

This may mean that you have simply made a typo entering the address – every dot and hyphen is critical, so just try again. If repeated tries return the same result and you are sure you have the correct address, the web server from which you are requesting the page might be down for some reason, so go somewhere else and come back to it in a while. If after a day or two of trying you still have no luck, it probably means the page has been taken down permanently.

Sometimes when you connect to your ISP and launch your browser you might be confronted with a blank screen. If going to other URLs also gives you a blank screen, but your computer tells you you're connected to the ISP, you might need to check if there's any link between your computer and the ISP by checking the connection box, which looks like this:

If you can see any change in the Bytes sent and Bytes received boxes, then you know they are talking, so just be patient. However, if the only box that's clicking over is the minutes and seconds spent on line, cut the connection and try again.

Bookmarking

If you find a page you think you'll use over and over, or a resource you don't really have time to read right now but would love to come back to, bookmark it for later reference. Bookmarking is Netscape-speak; Internet Explorer uses the word Favorites, but it's the same principle. Click on either Bookmarks or Favorites (depending on your browser) on the toolbar, and click on Add. This will store that URL for later use. To go back to a page you've bookmarked, simply go to the same button, and select the website from the drop-down list.

To send a useful resource to a friend, click once in the URL bar to select (highlight) the whole address, then click Copy, then create an e-mail and, once in the body of the e-mail, click Paste to drop the URL into the e-mail. Address the e-mail and send it on its way. Your friend will be able to copy and paste the URL into their own address bar, or launch the website directly from the e-mail if the e-mail package is sophisticated enough to read the address as a hyperlink.

PRINTING FROM BROWSERS

Printing from a browser is the same as printing from any other application, except that web pages are constructed on a frames structure, with multiple boxes, including advertisements, which you may not want to print. Look at the foot of the web page for the magic words: printer-friendly version. If the website has a printer-friendly option, take it, wait for the screen to refresh with the cut-down version, and then choose Print in the normal way. If the website doesn't offer a no-frills version, your printer will usually try and make a guess which frame you want, otherwise, you'll get the lot!

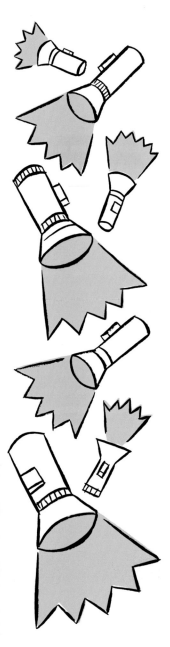

so it contains the two most important words: Norton and Upgrade, in that order. You'll have a better chance of the search engine understanding your request.

Becoming more specific

Adding extra words, separated by commas, can also help. So, for example, Recipes, Vegetarian, Broccoli will narrow your search results down to hopefully return a closer match than recipes for other things, like steak and kidney pie. Easiest of all is to use the + key between search words.

Just in case

In simple searches, case can be important; typing new zealand might not give the same results as New Zealand. However, if you use all upper case or all lower case, the search engine usually decides that case is not relevant. If case is important, use upper and lower to send the right message to your search engine, e.g., Museum of Modern Art, not MUSEUM OF MODERN ART.

Stems

Most search engines will automatically "stem" words so that if you type in the word Automate, it will also search for automatic, automated, automaton and other related words.

Quotation marks

If you don't want to include stemmed words in your search, enclose your search word in quotation marks, to restrict the search to that word only. This is useful for finding people, since typing Elvis Presley will find you Elvis Costello and Vernon Presley as well, whereas "Elvis Presley" should restrict the results to sites about the King.

Asterisks and question marks

To broaden the search without knowing a product's full name, or the spelling of a word, these punctuation marks can help. The number of question marks you add to the end of a string will substitute for that amount of missing information. Thus, Ford?? might find information about a Ford GT or a Ford XL, but not a Ford Coupe or a Ford Excel.

An asterisk represents multiple unknown characters, so cat* might return results on words which begin the same but are otherwise unrelated, e.g., cats, catalogue and catapults. If you're not sure what product you need from a particular family, it can be quite useful; Windows* should find information about Windows 95, Windows 98, Windows NT, Windows ME and Windows XP.

Boolean logic

Mathematician George Boole invented this logic stream; its principles are widely adopted in internet searches.

- Use OR to broaden your search; for example, red OR bird, to find information about the colour red and about birds.

- Use AND to narrow your search; for example, blue AND bonnet, to find information only about hats of that colour.

- Use NOT to restrict your search; for example, inkjet NOT laserjet, to find information about only one kind of printer.

More than one web

If you are at an interesting web page and want to open another one without leaving your current page, right click on the link you want to take, and select Open in New Window to open the new web page, while still keeping the existing page in another.

Buttons disappeared?

If you have accidentally lost the icons that get you around on the web (Back, Refresh, Home, etc), simply go to the View menu, choose Toolbars and click the box next to Standard Buttons to make sure it has a tick in it. Click OK and your buttons will reappear.

If Standard Buttons already has a tick next to it, that means the icons are on your desktop, they are just hiding. Look for a grey panel at the far right of the address bar, which is your icons bar shrunk down. Roll the cursor over until it turns into a two headed arrow, click and drag the bar out to size, and the icons will resume their place on the desktop.

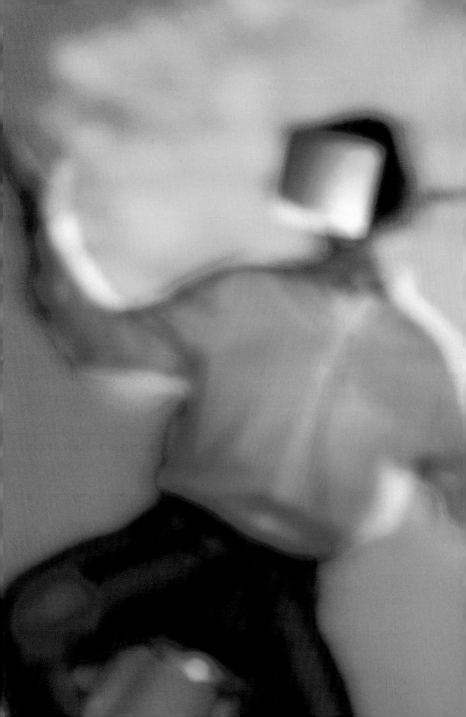

Stranger danger

Internet myths and real dangers

There are invariably stories that spring up concerning anything that's not well understood, and the internet has proven to be no exception.

The dark side of the internet is always talked about in terms of being a place rife with pornography, and lurking danger.

Remember, the internet doorway is a two-way medium – it lets you out into cyberspace, but it also lets information and, perhaps, malicious visitors in.

Home computers, although not immune, are not going to be targets of corporate crime, called cracking. Rather, your computer might, in a very unlikely scenario, become a target of a snooper who might like to see what's on your hard drive while you're connected to the internet, or fall victim to a virus. The likelihood of being snooped on rises and falls with your public profile; unless your name is Gates, Kidman or Cruise, it's unlikely that anyone will bother browsing through your hard drive for scandal and financial details. However, if it bothers you, buying and installing a simple internet security package should set your fears to rest. Designed to let you get out on the internet but stop anyone else getting in while the door is open, such software is a good investment in peace of mind.

No-one can infiltrate your computer if it is not connected to the internet.

IT'S ALL BABEL TO ME

Found something that looks interesting but you can't read because it's in another language? Let Babel Fish, an on-line translator, come to the rescue. Go to http://au.altavista.com/trns and either enter the text you'd like translated (cut and paste it) or type in the address of the website you'd like translated, and then click on the language-to-language option you need, say German to English, then click on the Translate button.

It's a machine translation, so you'll have to read between the lines on occasion, but the sense of the content is definitely there.

On the CD-ROM:
■ Filtering software to lend peace of mind about letting your kids onto the internet

Viruses and Trojan horses

Viruses and, to a lesser extent, Trojan horses, are the real dangers of being connected to the internet. A virus is a piece of maliciously written code which does damage to the operating system, applications and data on your hard drive. Maintaining up-to-date anti-virus software on your machine is a good investment, as is a little commonsense. Virus writers are increasingly resorting to social engineering to spread their nasty payloads, sending e-mail viruses titled "Read this because I Love You", or exhorting you to look at a picture of a famous person. Be wary of attachments, especially if they are from people you don't know.

A Trojan horse is a small intrusive applet that hides behind a legitimate attachment and buries itself into the workings of your computer. It can trigger a response at some future time or be activated to search out and report back on information it finds on your hard drive, while you're surfing the internet. A Trojan horse allows someone to take control of your computer remotely; the intruder can get in because you have a) opened the door by being on the internet, and b) let whoever it is plant the applet in your computer, albeit unknowingly. Again, the likelihood of this happening is in proportion to the importance of the information you have on your hard drive. If you use the computer for business-critical tasks, or keep other people's confidential information on it, make the investment in protecting yourself. Otherwise, relax, it will probably never happen. Home computer invasion is one of those dangers built into mythical proportions by a game of Chinese whispers.

Should I trust on-line friends?

More pertinent is the need to be careful about what you say to people you meet on line. Stories about people being conned and misled on line are common. More distressing are stories of children fooled by adults into revealing details about where they live, or being persuaded to meet these adults. Just because someone tells you their name, age and what they look like doesn't mean they are telling the truth.

Being able to create an on-line persona and reinvent yourself can be fun and, of course, it can be harmless, but it follows that you should treat everyone you meet on line as if they might be an invention, too.

And just as in real life you might find yourself the victim of a stalker, the phenomenon of cyberstalking is unfortunately also real. If you find yourself the focus of unwanted attention on line, don't go back to the same chat rooms or visit the forums the person might expect to find you in. Don't respond to messages, and don't be bludgeoned into giving information about yourself, or deceived into thinking that the person knows more about you than they actually do. No-one can find out where you live unless you tell them about yourself. If you have given a person your instant messaging identifier number, or e-mail address, and find yourself being harassed, change it. It's inconvenient, but it is also the simplest way of stopping the flow of unwanted messages.

If you find that you have given a person too much information about yourself and that person continues the harassment off-line, there are laws to protect you in the real world. Use them.

Dealing with on-line foes

http://www.cyberangels.com is an American-based group of cyber vigilantes whose mission is to make the internet a safer place, particularly for children. This website, staffed by volunteers, offers useful information about how to protect your children from on-line nasties, and also provides an e-mail Cyber 911 form, as a first port of call for reporting the experience of being harassed by a cyberstalker. Since the angels all live on line, the fact that it is a US-based organisation is irrelevant; they can help as if they were just around the corner.

Glossary

Applet a small but useful application, often serving just a single purpose.

Chatting "talking" in real time over the net, using a keyboard rather than your voice.

Compression technology for minimising the space a file occupies, to make it easier to store and faster to transmit.

Client describes the receiving computer, which calls information from a server, or information storage computer. A client is anything that receives information – a desktop, notebook, handheld, or even a mobile phone.

Cookie an applet sent by a website to your computer to gather data about you, such as your log-on details, and where you surfed immediately prior to coming to that site.

Cracker/Cracking someone who taps into other people's computers in order to steal information or do damage. Also commonly (but incorrectly) known as a hacker.

Cyberspace another word for the world of the internet.

Cyberstalking harassing someone on-line, bombarding someone's e-mail box with messages and behaving in an intrusive or threatening way.

Domain name a domain name locates an entity on the net and has three parts: the www (the location of the host server), the organisation identity and a suffix which indicates the purpose of the entity,

such as .com for a company or commercial enterprise, .gov for a government body, .edu for an educational institution, or .org for a non-profit body. Other extensions identify the country in which the domain is located, such as .au, or .nz. Simple .com extensions signify that the domain was registered in the US.

Download bring information from the net to your computer.

Expansion slot the space in your system unit to add extra internal devices, such as a modem or another hard drive.

Firewire a technology for adding peripherals to your computer, one that enhances the transmission speed of information, making it ideal for data-rich file transfers.

HTML (HyperText Markup Language) the code used to create web pages. HTML tells the user's browser what the page should look like and how to present the content.

HTTP (HyperText Transfer Protocol) used by a browser to seek web pages from a server.

Hyperlinks underlined links found in web pages that will transport you to a related page simply by clicking on them.

MP3 file format that will compress, store and play music.

Metatag keywords which describe the content of a website, designed as hooks for a search engine to bring people to that website.

Netizen a citizen of the net.

Newbie describes new users unfamiliar with the scope and conventions of the internet.

Off-line not connected to the internet.

On-line connected to the net.

Point to point security secures details of transactions across the net from the point of departure – your computer – to the website's server.

POP (Point Of Presence) the ISP connection dial-in point.

POP-based mail mail that is stored on the ISP's server until you download it. You can keep a copy on your hard drive, and view e-mails even when you're not connected.

Search engine software tool for helping you find useful relevant information on-line.

Server computer that stores information and forwards it on request to the "client".

Shareware software issued on a try-before-you-buy basis.

Shrinkwrapped boxed, wrapped software sold in stores. The word is used to distinguish this category from downloadable software, shareware and freeware.

TCP/IP the protocol, or set of instructions, used to ferry traffic across the internet.

Upload send information from your computer to the internet.

USB (Universal Serial Bus) a new connection technology for adding peripherals, such as a printer, to your computer.

URL (Universal Resource Locator) a website's address.

Web-based e-mail service in which your e-mail is stored on a service provider's server so you can access it from any computer with an up-to-date browser.

Index

Editor Julie Collard
Designer Alison Windmill
Illustrator Andrew Joyner
Photography Getty Images
Cover photography Sarah Callister
Screen shots Stuart McEacharn

ACP BOOKS STAFF
Editorial director Susan Tomnay
Creative director Hieu Nguyen
Publishing manager (sales)
Jennifer McDonald
Publishing manager (rights & new projects)
Jane Hazell

Production manager Carol Currie
Business manager Sally Lees

Chief executive officer John Alexander
Group publisher Jill Baker
Publisher Sue Wannan

Produced by ACP Books, Sydney.

Colour separations by
ACP Colour Graphics Pty Ltd, Sydney.
Printing by Dai Nippon Printing, Hong Kong.

Published by ACP Publishing Pty Limited,
54 Park St, Sydney; GPO Box 4088, Sydney,
NSW 1028. Ph: (02) 9282 8618
Fax: (02) 9267 9438.

acpbooks@acp.com.au
www.acpbooks.com.au

Australia Distributed by Network Services,
GPO Box 4088, Sydney, NSW 1028.
Ph: (02) 9282 8777 Fax: (02) 9264 3278.

United Kingdom Distributed by Australian
Consolidated Press (UK), Moulton Park
Business Centre, Red House Road,
Moulton Park, Northampton, NN3 6AQ.
Ph: (01604) 497 531
Fax: (01604) 497 533
acpukltd@aol.com

Canada Distributed by
Whitecap Books Ltd, 351 Lynn Ave,
North Vancouver, BC, V7J 2C4.
Ph: (604) 980 9852.

New Zealand Distributed by
Netlink Distribution Company, Level 4,
23 Hargreaves St, College Hill, Auckland 1.
Ph: (9) 302 7616.

South Africa Distributed by PSD Promotions
(Pty) Ltd, PO Box 1175, Isando 1600, SA.
Ph: (011) 392 6065.

Dancer, Helen.
The internet.

Includes index.
ISBN 1 86396 267 0

1. Internet. 2. World Wide Web.
I. Title. (Series: Australian Women's Weekly
Home Library). (Series: Computer basics).
004.678

© ACP Publishing Pty Limited 2002
ABN 18 053 273 546

This publication is copyright. No part of it
may be reproduced or transmitted in any
form without the written permission of the
publishers.

The publishers would like to thank
Samsung Australia Pty Ltd for props
used in photography.

Screen shots reprinted by permission from
Microsoft Corporation.

FAQs (Frequently Asked Questions)

How can I view the CD?

The CD attached to this book runs in a similar way to a website. To view the content, you need a web browser. Common browsers include Microsoft Internet Explorer (IE) and Netscape Communicator. Internet Explorer is pre-installed on all new computers.

What should I do if I don't have a web browser installed?

Don't worry, there are browsers for Windows and Mac available on the CD. For instructions on how to install one, read the file browser.txt located in the root directory of the CD.

Do I need to connect to the internet to use the CD?

No, you do not have to be on the internet to view the contents of the CD and install the software found on the CD. Everything is included on the CD.

Can the CD run on my system?

The CD runs on any machine running Windows 95, Windows 98, Windows ME, Windows XP, Mac OS 9 and Mac OS X. Individual programs and demos on the disc have their own system requirements, which may be higher.

How do I get started?

WINDOWS USERS: Place this CD into the CD-ROM drive and the home page will open up automatically. **NB:** If the CD does not start after 30 seconds, double-click My Computer on your desktop, then the CD icon and then Default.

MAC USERS: Load the CD then double-click on the CD icon that appears on screen, to launch the contents list. Click on Default to open the home page.

How do I use the CD?

Once the home page appears, click on the link "How to use the CDs" for a quick tutorial. Also see "What's on the CDs".

What do I do if I have a problem?

We are happy to provide written technical support for using the CD, but are unable to provide telephone support, or any support for the third-party software on the disc. If you have questions about the CD, contact us via e-mail at acpbooks@acp.com.au or send mail to ACP Books, GPO Box 4088, Sydney, NSW 1028. Alternatively, you can fax us on (02) 9267 9438. Please include details of the problem and a return address, e-mail address (if available) and daytime telephone number so that we can contact you. If your CD is faulty, please contact us for a replacement on (02) 9282 8618. For further help and the latest information, please read the file ReadMe.txt located in the root directory of the CD.